Around the Table with Family and Friends

Letitia Fernandez

DEDICATION

This book is dedicated to my mother. She has shown me that a strong woman can work and still take care of her family and home after a long day of work and still produce a decent meal for her family.

These cooking inspirations came from my mother. Both my parents had to work but even after a long day she managed to still come home and make a beautiful dinner. My father was in the military and my mother did jobs that had her away from home for 8 hours. My mother would walk in the kitchen, still in her work clothes, and kick off her heels to start dinner. When we sat down to eat it would be the best comfort food with dinner done under an hour! I am talking about meat, starch, vegetable or salad and from time to time dinner rolls, okay!

Dinner time is most important to me and my family because it gives us time to connect with one another about how our days have gone. It gives my husband and I time to ask the kids about school, current events or life issues that at this time is super important (Covid-19 lockdown). This is our bonding time with no cell phones at the table. Just us being able to have time to speak our minds and enjoy one another. I have to remind myself life is too short and our kids grow up fast, so enjoy this time with them as much as you can.

Anytime I hear of any of my family members having a bad day I would try to make their special meal as I feel it's medicine for the soul. Seeing their smiles back warms my heart as much as my meals warm their stomachs. I love my family and love to whip up a great meal!

CONTENTS

ACKNOWLEDGMENTS

I would like to thank my loving husband, Michael for pushing me to write this cookbook. I love you and appreciate you.

To my children and bonus children, may you have this book on your shelf in your home and have great family times in generations to come. I love you all!

Meats

3 PACK POT ROAST INSTANT POT
COOK TIME 1 HOUR 30 MINS

Ingredients:

1 3lb beef roast (Chuck and Rump roast are delicious as well.)
1 packet of Ranch Powder Seasoning
1 packet of Italian Power Dressing
2 packs of Brown Gravy
3 packs of Sazon
1 cup of water
1 tbsp. cornstarch
1 small onion (chopped)
Carrots (if desired, chopped)

1. Turn the Instant Pot on to sauté and brown the onions and add the meat to brown on both sides.

2. Sprinkle both brown gravy packs, ranch pack, Italian seasoning pack, and Sazon packs over the   roast.

3. Add water

4. Place the lid on top and be sure the seal is closed and press manual high pressure for 90mintues on high or click on meat/stew, click on high and set the time for 90 mins

5. Do a release for 15 mins to allow the pressure out of the pot then Carefully remove the lid.

6. Use a fork to shred the meat while in the pot with the Au Jus.

7. Serve over rice or potatoes and drizzle the gravy over the top to ENJOY!

Wings

Cook Time 20 minutes

<u>Ingredients:</u>

1 pound of Chicken Wings

2 packs of Sazon (Goya)

1tsp Garlic seasoning

1tbsp of Adobo seasoning

1. In a large bowl add chicken and season the meats with all of the ingredients
2. Mix well and place a saran wrap over chicken and place in the fridge for 1 hour.
3. In a large skillet add vegetable oil to pan and place on medium to high heat
4. Wait for the oil to warm up and place the chicken wings in the pan, cooking each side for 10 minutes.
5. Once chicken is done place on a napkin to get the excess grease off the meat.
6. You can either eat the wings plain or try the sauce below.

Asian Dipping sauce for the wings

Prep Time 5 minutes

Ingredients:

½ tsp of Sesame Seed Oil

⅛ cup Thai style Sweet Chili sauce

¼ cup Szechuan Spicy Sauce

1. Mix well and either dip the wings in the sauce or drizzle the sauce over the wings

BEEF TIPS AND GRAVY
COOK TIME 1 HOUR AND 45 MINS

<u>Ingredients:</u>

2 lbs. of cubed chuck steak or stew meat
2 tablespoons Olive Oil
1 Onion Chopped
3 packs of Brown Gravy
1 tbsp. of Adobo seasoning
3 packs of Sazon seasoning
3 ½ cups of Water
1 Bay Leaf
Salt & Pepper to taste
2 tbsp. of minced garlic
1/3 cup of Red Wine (if desired)

1. In a large pot or Dutch oven, 2 tablespoon of Olive Oil over medium to high heat.

2. Add Garlic to sauté

3. Add Onion to sauté

4. Place meat in pot and allow to brown by stirring constantly

5. Add Brown Gravy, Adobo seasoning, Sazon seasoning and water.

6. Bring to a boil for 5 mins and then place on medium to low heat.

7. If you want to thicken your gravy add cornstarch with 1/3 cup water and pour into the pot a little at a time while stirring constantly until you get your desired consistency.

8. Serve over rice, pasta noodles, or mashed potatoes to Enjoy!

SALISBURY STEAK
COOK TIME 1 HOUR AND 45 MINUTES

Ingredients:

Combined all in a big bowl and mix with hands to make small hamburger patties
1 lb of ground beef
½ cup of Italian Breadcrumbs
3 packs of sazon seasoning
1 egg
2 tbsp ketchup
1/4 cup of steak seasoning
1/3 cup of heavy whipping cream

Gravy
5oz mushrooms (sliced)
½ cup of onion chopped
1 tsp of minced garlic
2 packs for brown powdered gravy packs
2 ½ cups of water

1. Add olive oil to a pan over medium-high heat. Add patties and cook the first side for 2 minutes or until brown, then flip to the other side until brown.

2. Take patties out of pan and place on a platter or plate

3. Add olive oil to pan and add ½ onion chopped and ½ tbsp. of garlic, sautéed

4. Add mushrooms into the pan for 2-3 minutes until golden brown

5. Turn heat to medium add 2 brown gravy packs (powered) with 2 ½ cups of water

6. Add steaks along with the juice from the plate into the pan with the gravy and allow to cook on medium heat for 5-7 mins. or until the gravy is thick but stir around the steaks. If gravy is too thick you can add more water.

7. Serve Salisbury steak with potatoes and add Salt & Pepper to taste.

Enjoy!

CUBED STEAKS WITH RED SAUCE
COOK TIME 45 MINUTES

Ingredients:

1 pack of cubed steaks
1 can of diced tomatoes (14.5oz can)
1 jar of Sofrito (12oz)
4 packs of Sazon
1 tbsp. of adobo seasoning
1 tsp. of garlic
Salt & Pepper to taste

1. Add olive oil to the pan over medium-high heat.

2. Place the cubed steak in pan and sprinkle adobo seasoning on both sides of the meat

3. Add garlic

4. Cook on both sides 2-3 minutes or until brown

5. Add in can of diced tomatoes and jar of Sofrito

6. Place on medium heat while stirring around the meat

7. Allow to cook on each side for 7-10 minutes

8. You can take out the cubes and cut into strips if you desire and place back in the red sauce

9. Great with rice and green beans. Enjoy!

PORK CHOPS
COOK TIME 45 MINUTES

Ingredients:

1 pack of pork chops (5-6 chops on the tray)
1/8 cup of Adobo seasoning
4 packs of Sazon seasoning
1 tbsp. Paprika

1. Season chops and place in a baking pan.

2. Preheat the oven to 350.

3. Place chops in the oven and cook for 45 minutes, halfway through turn over the chops and remain cooking until the time is complete

4. This would be good with a toss salad.

Enjoy!

Ground Beef Taco Meat
Cook Time 25 minutes

Ingredients:

2lbs of ground beef taco meat
3 fresh roman tomatoes (cut up)
1 small yellow onion
1 tsp of mines garlic
¼ cup of steak seasoning (Fiesta Steak Seasoning is my preference)
¼ cup of water

In a pan brown the ground beef and cook until brown and you see no more red.
Drain oil off meat and add the meat back to the same pan
Add steak seasoning
Add tomatoes, onion, garlic
Add water and continue to stir until the onions and tomatoes are cooked

This would be great to serve in Tacos or as pictured.
Just add all of your condiments
Great with Spanish rice and beans

Letitia's Simple Guacamole
Mix Time 10 minutes

Ingredients:

2 large avocados
1tbsp salt

1. Cut avocados into a bowl

2. Smash with a fork

3. Add in salt

4. Mix well

ENJOY!

Pork Tenderloin with a creamy white sauce
Cook Time 35 minutes

Ingredients:

1 tsp sea salt
½ tsp freshly ground pepper
1 tsp garlic

1. Mix all seasonings and rub on the tenderloin.

2. In a large pan heat 1tsp oil over medium heat, once oil is hot. Add pork and brown on all sides (total of 8 minutes)

3. Remove tenderloin from the pan and slice in 1 ½ thick and place it back into a hot pan. If you need to drizzle a little bit of more olive oil this will be ok. Cook for 35 minutes until the pork is done and you don't see any more pink.

4. In another pan you will be making the creamy white sauce so you and smother the tenderloin in it.

Easy Alfredo Sauce
Cook Time 20 minutes

<u>Ingredients:</u>

1./2 c. butter
1 ½ c. heavy whipping cream
2 tsp minced garlic
½ tsp salt
½ tsp pepper
2 cups freshly grated parmesan cheese

1. Add butter and cream into large skillet

2. Simmer over low heat for 2 minutes

3. Whisk in the garlic, salt and pepper for 1 minute

4. Whisk in the parmesan cheese until melted

5. After the pork is done take the alfredo sauce and pour it in the same pan as the tenderloin. Allowing it to Smoother and place on low heat for 30 minutes.

Enjoy!

Easy Chicken Cacciatore
Cook Time 40 minutes

Ingredients:

6 boneless skinless Chicken Breast cut into strips
One Green Pepper cut thin sliced
1 medium Onion, diced
1 small Yellow Bell Pepper, diced
1 small red Bell Pepper, diced
1 large carrot, peeled and sliced
10 oz. Mushrooms, sliced
1/2 cup pitted Black Olives
8 sprigs Thyme
2 tablespoons each freshly chopped parsley and basil plus more to garnish
1 teaspoon dried Oregano
150 ml Red Wine
28 oz. Canned crushed T
2 tablespoons tomato paste
7 oz. Roma Tomatoes, halved
1/2 teaspoon Red Pepper Flakes

1. Season the chicken with salt and pepper then Heat 2 tablespoons oil in either a large pot or pan. Sear chicken on both sides until golden, about 3-4 minutes each side. Remove from the skillet and set aside.

2. Add remaining oil to the pan. Sauté the onion until transparent, about 3-4 minutes. Add in garlic and cook until fragrant, about 30 seconds. Add the peppers, carrot, mushrooms and herbs; cook for 5 minutes until vegetables begin to soften. Pour in the wine, scraping up browned bits from the bottom of the skillet. Cook until wine is reduced, about 2 minutes.

3. Add crushed tomatoes, tomato paste, Roma tomatoes and chill flakes. Season with salt and pepper to your tastes. Return chicken pieces to the skillet and continue to cook over stove top.

4. Mix all of the ingredients together; cover with lid, reduce heat to low and allow to simmer (while stirring occasionally) for 40 minutes or until the meat is falling apart. Add in the olives, allow to simmer for a further 10 minutes. Garnish with parsley. Great with Rice, or egg noodles. Enjoy!

Korean style short ribs
Cook Time 5 minutes

<u>Ingredients:</u>

3 pounds of Short Ribs flank style (Kalbi)
1/3 cup of Soy Sauce
1/3 cup of Teriyaki Sauce
1/8 cup of minced Garlic
1 tablespoon Sesame Oil
2 packs of Sazon

1. Either in a large Tupperware or gallon size Ziploc place rib flank with soy sauce, teriyaki sauce, minced garlic, sesame oil and 2 packs of Sazon

2. Allow to marinate for 24 hours

3. Ideal to make on the grill but you can sear in a skillet on the stove

4. Cook on each side for 2-5 minutes until nicely browned but juicy. Place the meat on a platter and serve right away.

Enjoy!

Adobo Chicken
Cook Time 40 minutes

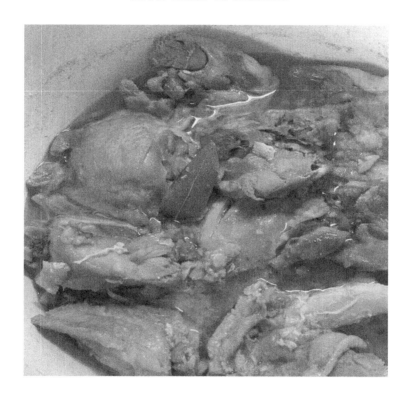

<u>Ingredients:</u>

2 tsp Olive Oil
3 pounds of Chicken Thighs
1 large Onion, sliced
2 tsp Minced Garlic
1/3 c White Vinegar
2/3 c Soy Sauce
2 tsp Black Pepper
1 Bay Leaf

1. Heat the large skillet over medium-high heat.

2. Cook the chicken thighs until the chicken is golden brown on all sides.

3. In the same pot stir garlic and onion and cook until it's soft roughly for 5 minutes.

4. Pour in vinegar, soy sauce, black pepper and bay leaf.

5. Place the temperature to medium-low, cover and simmer for 35-40 minutes.

Enjoy!

Shredded Pork
Cook Time 4-5 hours

Ingredients:

8-10 lbs. Pork Shoulder
½ c Vegetable Oil
½ tsp of Minced Garlic
3 packages of Sazon (Goya)
Adobo seasoning
1/3 c. Soy Sauce
1/3 c. Teriyaki Sauce

1. Rinse your Pork Shoulder the night before rinse the pork shoulder the you can either use a cooking bag to marinate the meat or you can seal the meat in a cooking pan and seal with foil.

2. Good to marinade for 24 hours.

3. Add holes to the meat to place the minced garlic inside.

4. Take the remaining ingredients and sprinkle or pour over the shoulder.

5. This takes 4 to 5 hours to cook depending on the size and your oven so you must time yourself on the time you want it done. I typically place this in the oven either in the morning or around lunchtime.

6. For the first two hours set your oven at 275 Fahrenheit and allow it to cook covered.

7. After two hours turn the pork over and sit at 350 Fahrenheit and continue cooking for two hours or more uncovered.

Enjoy!

Sides

Creamy Spinach
Cook Time 7-9 minutes

Ingredients:

20oz of Baby Spinach
2 tbsp. Butter
½ medium Onion, Chopped
½ cup of Heavy Whipping Cream
4 oz. of Cream Cheese
¼ cup Fresh Grated Parmesan Cheese
¼ cup Romano Cheese
Salt and Pepper to taste

1. In a large pot of boiling water, cook spinach for 30 seconds.

2. Drain and place in a bowl with ice water. When the spinach is cool, drain and squeeze out as much water as you can.

3. In a large skillet over medium to high heat, melt butter.

4. Add onions and cook for 5 minutes or until soft. Add garlic until fragrant for 1 minute.

5. Add heavy whipping cream and cream cheese to the pan. Simmer to low until cream cheese is melted.

6. Season with salt and pepper for taste.

7. Add spinach, parmesan and Romano cheese and stir to combine all ingredients.

Enjoy!

Crispy Potatoes
Cook Time 15 minutes

Ingredients:

1lb, baby potatoes, halved
1 tbsp. extra-virgin olive oil
1 tsp. garlic powder
1 tsp. Italian seasoning
Salt and pepper to taste

1. In large bowl, toss potatoes with oil, garlic powder, and Italian seasoning

2. Place potatoes on parchment paper onto of the baking sheet place even layer

3. Bake on 425 F for 15 minutes or until crispy- remove the pan from the oven and flip the potatoes halfway through.

4. Rearrange again so that the potatoes are evenly spaced and not overlapping.

5. Then bake for 10-15 more minutes, or until the potatoes are tender and have begun to brown and caramelize a bit around the edges.

6. Remove baking sheeting from the oven and sprinkle salt and pepper for taste.

7. If desired (sprinkle fresh parmesan cheese)

Enjoy!

Green Bean Casserole with Bacon in the Air Fryer
Cook Time 13 minutes

1c. Cream of Mushrooms Soup
½ c. Milk
½ tsp Soy Sauce
¼ tsp. Freshly Ground Pepper
2/3 c. French's Fried Onions
3 1/2c. trimmed Green Beans, blanched and cooled
1 pack of Bacon

1. In a large mixing bowl, stir together cream of mushrooms, milk, soy sauce, pepper and French's fried onions.

2. Add green beans and toss in the bowl.

3. Cut the bacon slices in halves

4. Grab a small bundle of green beans and wrap with a strip of bacon

5. Working in batches, place bundles seam side down in the air fryer
6. Cook at 375 for 12-13 minutes or until the bacon is crispy.

Enjoy!

Brussels Sprout Chips
Cook Time 8-10 minutes

Ingredients:

1/2 lb. Brussel Sprouts, thinly sliced
1 tbsp. Extra-Virgin Olive Oil
2 tbsp. Fresh Parmesan Cheese and will add more to garnish
1 tsp. Garlic Powder
Salt and Pepper

1. Preheat the oven to 400. In a large bowl toss sprouts with oil, parmesan, garlic powder and season with salt and pepper.

2. Spread evenly on parchment paper onto of the baking sheet place even layer.

3. Bake for 10 minutes, then toss and back for an additional 8-10 more until crisp and golden.

4. Garnish with more Parmesan cheese.

Enjoy!

Twice Baked Potato Casserole
Cook Time 35 minutes

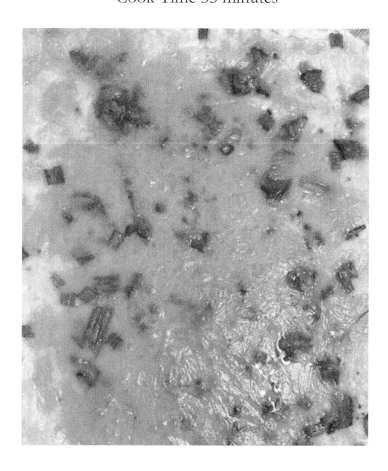

Ingredients:

6 large Russet Potatoes
4 tbsp. Butter, softened, plus more later for the pan
4 oz. of Cream Cheese, softened
1 c. Sour Cream
1 1/2c of Heavy Whipping Cream
2 ¾ c Shredded Cheddar
10 slices of Bacon, Cooked and chopped
5 Green Onions, chopped
¾ tsp Garlic Powder
Salt and Pepper for taste

1. Preheat the oven to 400. Remove the skin from the potatoes and then place potatoes in a large pot with water and cook until the potatoes are tender. Drained water off potatoes and place them in a large bowl

2. Mashed and added butter, cream cheese, sour cream, and heavy whipping cream. Stir until the butter and cream cheese are melted. Fold in cheese, 2 quarters of bacon, 2 quarters of green onions and garlic powder. Season with salt and pepper for taste.

3. Spray the baking pan with spray oil and transfer the mixture into the baking dish.
4. Sprinkle the remaining cheese to the top

5. Bake until cheese is melted for about 20 minutes, turn on broil for 2-3 minutes until the top is golden brown. Let cool for 8-10 minutes.

6. Add remaining bacon and green onions.

Enjoy!

Steam Broccoli
Cook Time 15 minutes

2 lbs. of frozen broccoli (fresh or frozen)

1. In a large skillet add 1tbsp of water over medium heat

2. Place broccoli in pan and cover with a lid for 10-15 minutes (steaming)

3. Add salt and pepper for taste

Enjoy!

Letitia's Marinara Red Sauce
Cook Time 35minutes

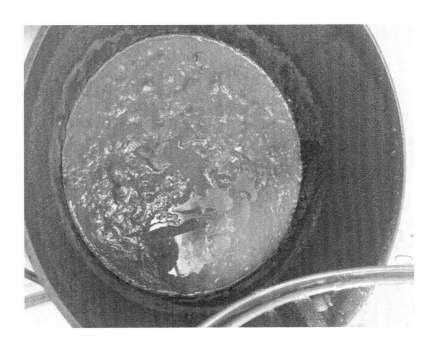

Ingredients:

2 tbsp. Olive Oil
1 tbsp. Minced Garlic
½ c. Onion, Chopped
5 Roma Tomatoes, peeled and chopped
1 ½ tbsp. fresh Basil finely chopped
2 c. Tomato Sauce
1 teaspoon Oregano
Salt and Pepper to taste

1. Heat oil in pot on medium heat

2. Add onions and garlic and cook for 5minutes

3. Add tomatoes, basil, tomato sauce, oregano, salt and pepper, combined and stir

4. Simmer for 25-30 minutes

5. **For easy tomato peeling you can Blanch them. Add tomatoes to boiling water, cook for 1-2 minutes, then immediately place in ice water to stop cooking.

6. If desired, you can add in cooked and drained ground beef to the sauce

Easy Alfredo Sauce
Cook Time 10-12 minutes

1./2 c. butter
1 ½ c. heavy whipping cream
2 tsp minced garlic
½ tsp salt
½ tsp pepper
2 cups freshly grated parmesan cheese

1. Add butter and cream into large skillet

2. Simmer over low heat for 2 minutes

3. Whisk in the garlic, salt and pepper for 1 minute

4. Whisk in the parmesan cheese until melted

5. Served and Enjoy

6. *If desired you can add in ¼ c of pesto sauce* mix well
7.

Mom's mashed potatoes
Cook Time 25 minutes

Ingredients:

2 lbs russet or Idaho potatoes
2 tsp salt
3 tbsp unsalted butter
1/3 c mayonnaise
1/3 c milk
1tbsp garlic
½ cup of parmesan

1. Wash and peel the potatoes and cut into 1-inch cubes.

2. Place into a large pot with water. Add 2 tsp of salt and bring to boil.

3. Cook for 20 minutes until the potatoes are tender when you pierce with a fork.

4. Drain potatoes and return to the same pot.

5. Mashed potatoes with masher to your liking.

6. Add butter, mayo, garlic, parmesan and milk.

7. Mix well and add more mix if necessary, to get the smooth consistency.

8. Add salt to taste.

ENJOY!

Jasmine rice with a rice cooker
Cook Time 20 minutes

Rinse the rice several times until your water runs clear. Failure to do so will result in your rice being sticky.

After washing the jasmine rice and drain the water off, place it in the rice cooker.

1tsp of salt

Water to rice ratio for a rice cooker 1:1
For example
1 cup of rice will use 1 cup of water
2 cups of rice will use 2 cups of water
whatever cup you use on the rice, use that same cup for the water. DO NOT use a different cup
Set the rice cooker setting.
My rice cooker has a quick cook and that's what I use but I have other settings. It usually takes 20 minutes to cook the rice

Once the rice is done cooking, wait 10 minutes before opening the lid.

Fluff the rice and it's ready to eat. ENJOY!

If you decide to cook the rice on the stove the ration for example is the following:

1 cup of rice will use 1.5 cups of water

2 cups of rice will use 2/5 cups of water

Whatever cup you use to measure the rice will be the same cup to measure the water

Let the rice cook for 20 minutes over medium-low heat

Wait 10 minutes and after 20 minutes go ahead and turn off the heat and wait for 10 minutes before opening the lid.

Fluff the rice and it's ready to eat. ENJOY!

Sheron's Red Rice
Cook Time 25 minutes

<u>Ingredients:</u>

1 c. long grain rice
2.c water
14.5oz Hunt's diced tomatoes

1. Rinse the rice several times until your water runs clear. Failure to do so will result in your rice being sticky

2. Place the rice in the pot with the 2 cups of water and add 1tsp of salt

3. Cook the rice (20 minutes) until the rice is almost done but still has a little bit of water in the pot

4. 4 tbsp. of margarine stir in the rice

5. Pour the entire can of diced tomatoes in the pot. Stir well and turn off and remove from the burner.

6. Add tsp salt

Enjoy!

<u>Why I love this rice:</u>
As a child my mother would make this all the time for us growing up. There would be times I could have a bad day and come home from school and my mother would have made this scrumptious red rice and paired it with pork chops and green beans. I guess my mother would know the type of day we were having and wanted to make sure we had a nice comfort food to take our mind off of our kid-life problems.

Egg Roll filling
Cook Time 35 minutes

Ingredients:

1 lb of ground beef
1 bag 3 color deli coleslaw (14oz)
1 bag of bean sprout (12oz)
1/8 soy sauce
1/3 sesame oil

1. In a large skillet cook the ground beef until entirely done.

2. Drain the oil off the beef and place back in the same pan.

3. Add 1 bag of coleslaw, and one bag of bean sprouts to the skillet with the ground beef.

4. Allow to cook and add 1/8 soy sauce, and 1/3 sesame oil.

5. Allow to cook until the coleslaw and beansprouts are soft.

6. Great to place over steam white rice.

Enjoy!

Salads

I love to make these salads every summer especially because it brings back memories of living in Hawaii as a teenager. I have now passed this on to my children who love to have these special salads in the summer months. From my Family to yours...Enjoy!

__Berry Salad__
Prep Time 15 minutes

Ingredients:

2lb strawberry
1lb blueberry
1lb blackberry

1. Wash the strawberries and slice in fours

2. Wash blueberry and blackberry

3. Combine all fruit in a large bowl mix with a large spoon

4. Sprinkle 1/3 tsp of sugar or honey on top of the fruit.

Enjoy!

Fruit Salad
Prep Time 15 minutes

1lb strawberry
1lb blueberry
1lb blackberry
½ lb. of green grapes
1 20oz can of pineapples

1. Wash strawberries and slice in fours

2. Wash grapes and slice in half

3. Wash blueberry and blackberry

4. Drain the pineapple juice from the can

5. Combine all fruit in a large bowl mix with a large spoon

6. Sprinkle 1/3 tsp of sugar or honey on top of the fruit.

Enjoy!

Ceviche
Prep Time 20 minutes

1 pound cooked shrimp
¼ c red onion
2 avocado
½ c fresh cilantro
¼ c fresh lime juice
½ c orange juice
4 whole Romano tomatoes
If desired 2 whole jalapeno peppers if you want a kick

1. Chop the shrimp into ½ inch pieces and place in a large bowl

2. In a small bowl whisk together lime, and orange juice and pour over shrimp.

3. Allow to sit for 15 minutes before you add the ingredients below.

4. Diced tomatoes, chopped jalapeno peppers, chopped cilantro, and finely chopped red onion, and placed in the bowl with the shrimp.

5. Marinade for 10 minutes.

6. Add dice avocado.

7. Season the ceviche with salt and pepper for taste. Enjoy!

Squash, Zucchini and broccoli
Cook Time 10-15 minutes

Ingredients:

1 squash (cut in chunks)
1 zucchini (cut in chunks)
3 cups of frozen broccoli (or fresh)

1. In a large skillet place on medium to high heat

2. Add drizzle of olive oil

3. Place all zucchini, broccoli and squash in pan

4. Stir for a few minutes 5 minutes and then place lid to steam the vegetables
5. place the heat on low-medium heat for 5-7 minutes

6. add salt and pepper to taste

Enjoy!

Zucchini, Squash and Asparagus
Cook Time 10-15 minutes

Ingredients:

1 zucchini (cut in chunks)
1 squash (cut in chucks)
1 stack of asparagus (cut in half)

1. In a large skillet place on medium to high heat

2. add drizzle of olive oil

3. place all zucchini, asparagus and squash in pan

4. stir for a few minutes (5minutes) and then place lid to steam the vegetables

5. place the heat on low-medium heat (5-7 minutes)

6. add salt and pepper to taste

Enjoy!

Quick Tips!

Quick Tip

Did you know you can freeze butter? It's true!

When you see a sale on butter (especially sticks for baking) grab a bunch. Come home and freeze them!

Use as needed.

Did you know if you lightly spray or wipe oil in the measuring container before you pour the honey in, it will slide out easier and quicker!!!

Use the Right Onion

USES OF LEMON PEEL

Did you know?
Lemon peels contain as much as 5 to 10 times more vitamins than the lemon juice itself.

- Cancer
- Bone Health
- Oral Health and Hygiene
- Weight loss
- Internal parasites and worms
- Bacterial infections and fungi
- Antidepressant
- Regulate blood pressure
- Cysts and tumors
- Rich source of vitamin C
- Deodorize garbage disposal
- Keep insects out
- Acne

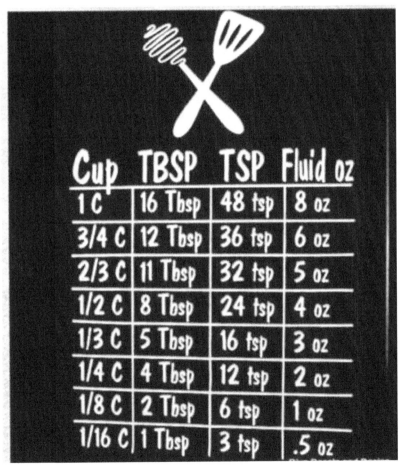

Cup	TBSP	TSP	Fluid oz
1 C	16 Tbsp	48 tsp	8 oz
3/4 C	12 Tbsp	36 tsp	6 oz
2/3 C	11 Tbsp	32 tsp	5 oz
1/2 C	8 Tbsp	24 tsp	4 oz
1/3 C	5 Tbsp	16 tsp	3 oz
1/4 C	4 Tbsp	12 tsp	2 oz
1/8 C	2 Tbsp	6 tsp	1 oz
1/16 C	1 Tbsp	3 tsp	.5 oz

ABOUT THE AUTHOR

I am a wife and mother of five children and three fur babies. I made the decision when I was a young adult to take a jab in the travel industry since I loved vacations and making memories with family and friends. I have traveled all over the world from Europe, Canada, many parts of the US and the Caribbean islands. I love to eat, so of course when you are in various parts of the world I would enjoy a nice dinner at well-known or maybe top rated restaurants. I have always been fascinated with the presentation, cooking styles and the flavors that make the meals taste so good. My husband has shared with me when we visit a restaurant and we enjoy a meal that I always come home and try to make the same dish.

I just love to cook and feed the soul.

Made in the USA
Monee, IL
12 October 2020

44545578R00037